100 QUESTIONS AND ANSWERS

GW01465185

Undisco
Life on Earth

Written by
Phil Gates

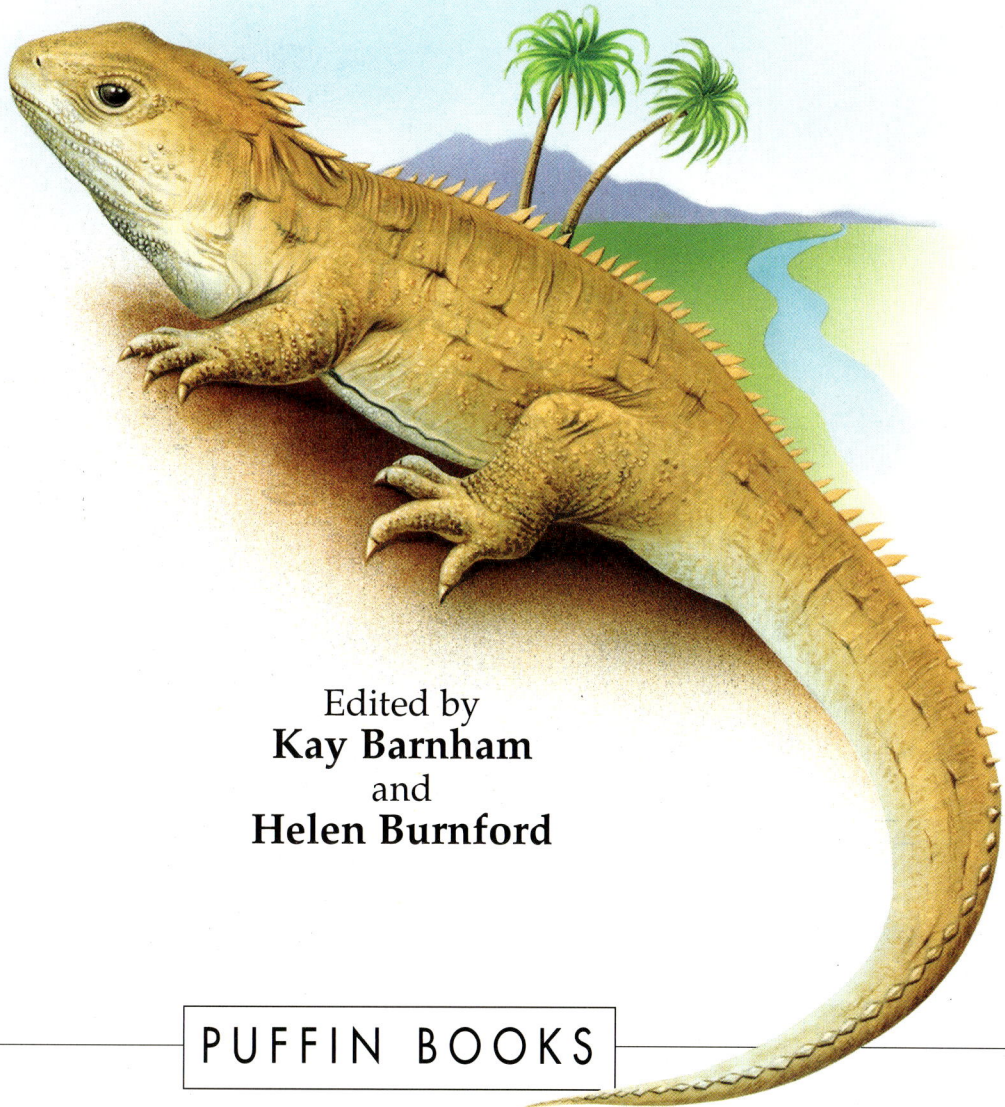

Edited by
Kay Barnham
and
Helen Burnford

PUFFIN BOOKS

The author, Phil Gates is a Lecturer in Botany at Durham University. He has written several science books for children.

Celia Wilson, the consultant, has a Hons degree in Zoology and has worked for London University Biology departments.

PUFFIN BOOKS

Published by the Penguin Group
Penguin Books Ltd, 27 Wrights Lane, London W8 5TZ, England
Penguin Books USA Inc., 375 Hudson Street, New York, New York 10014, USA
Penguin Books Australia Ltd, Ringwood, Victoria, Australia
Penguin Books Canada Ltd, 10 Alcorn Avenue, Toronto, Ontario, Canada M4V 3B2
Penguin Books (NZ) Ltd, 182-190 Wairau Road, Auckland 10, New Zealand

Penguin Books Ltd, Registered Offices: Harmondsworth, Middlesex, England

First published 1996
10 9 8 7 6 5 4 3 2 1

Copyright © 1996 Zigzag Publishing Ltd
All rights reserved

Produced for Puffin Books by Zigzag Publishing Ltd, The Barn, Randolph's Farm, Brighton Road, Hurstpierpoint, West Sussex, BN6 9EL, England

Creative Manager: Hazel Songhurst
Editorial Manager: Helen Burnford
Production: Zoë Fawcett and Simon Eaton
Designed by: Kate Buxton
Illustrated by: Peter Bull Studios, Peter Dennis and Guy Smith, Mainline Design
Cover design: Nicky Chapman
Cover illustration: Michael Steward
Series concept: Tony Potter

Colour separations: Pendry Litho, Hove, England.
Printed by: Proost, Belgium

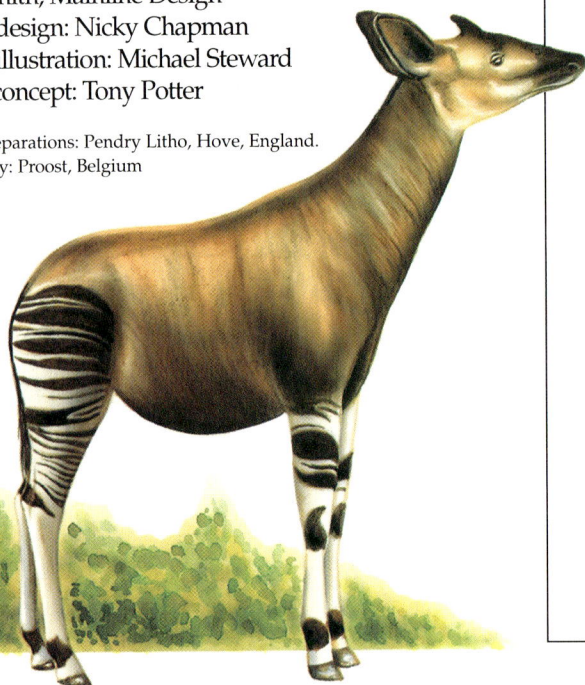

Contents

About this book

This book answers all your questions about the amazing creatures that are still being discovered in distant parts of the world. Scientists believe that at least 30 million species of plants and animals share Planet Earth with us, but so far they have only found about one and a half million. You can read how new species are discovered, and learn how you can become a scientist who searches for undiscovered life.

Where do scientists go to search for undiscovered animals? What strange animals live around underwater volcanoes in the deepest parts of the oceans? Where were megamouth sharks and komodo dragons first discovered? Could apemen and the Loch Ness monster really exist? Can genetic engineers recreate extinct species? These are just a few of the questions that will be answered as you turn these pages.

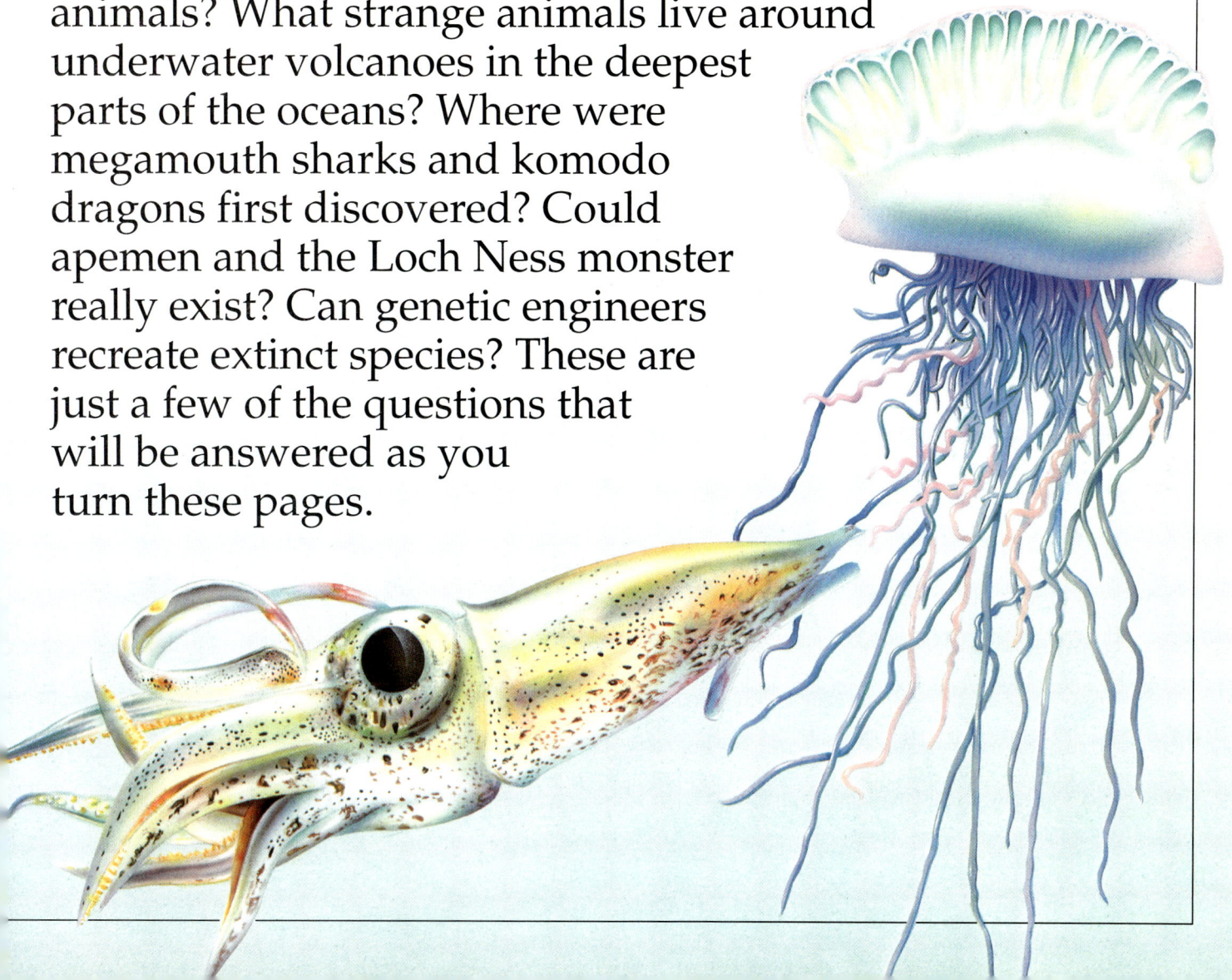

Although we cannot be certain how many exist, some scientists think there may only be 10 million species.

How many living things exist?

The living world is made up of different types of animals, plants, fungi, protozoans (single-celled animals), algae (single-celled plants), bacteria and viruses. Scientists who try to describe and classify them all still do not know how many exist.

Q What is a species?

A A species is a group of living things that is different from all other living things. Sometimes the differences are very small. Individuals of a species can usually only breed with their own kind.

Indian python

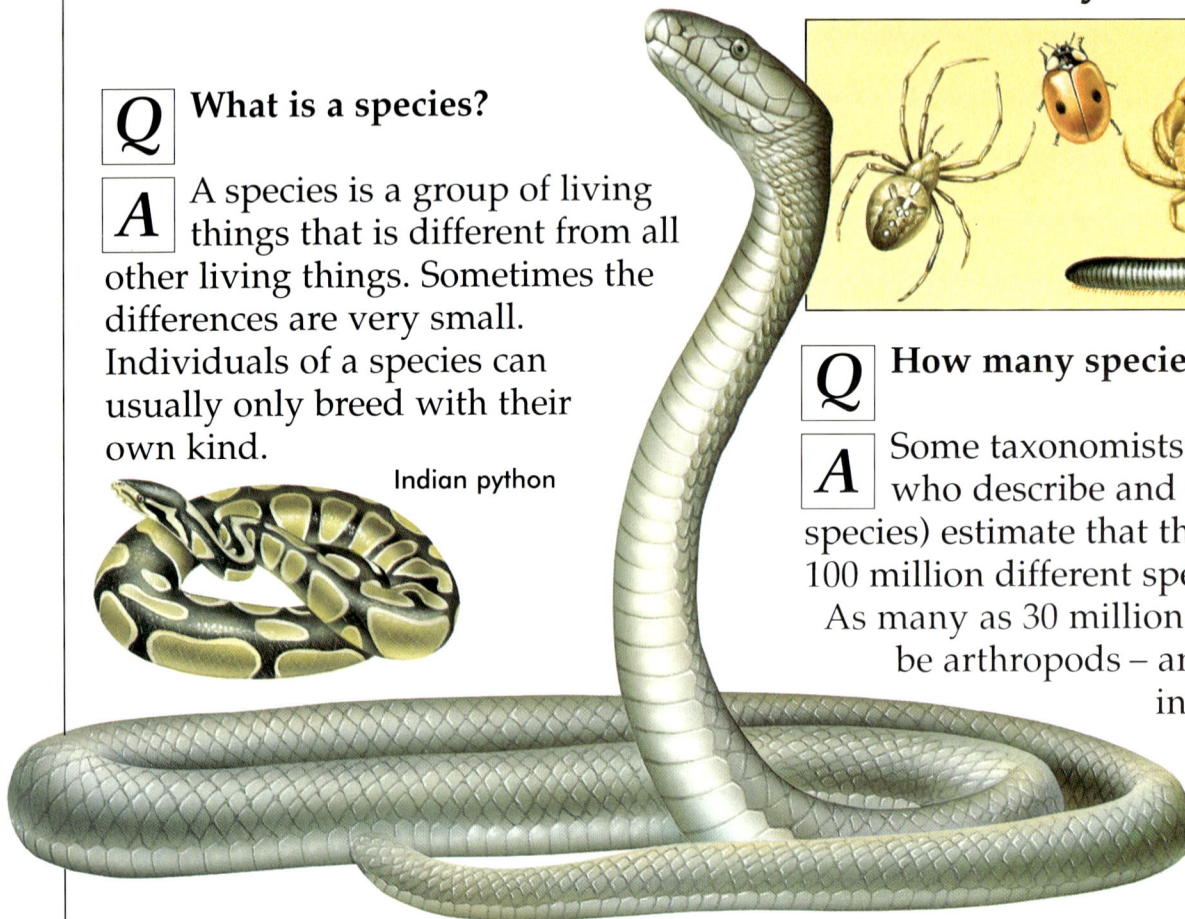

Q How many species are there?

A Some taxonomists (scientists who describe and classify new species) estimate that there may be 100 million different species on Earth. As many as 30 million species could be arthropods – animals such as insects, spiders, crabs and millipedes.

Boa constrictor

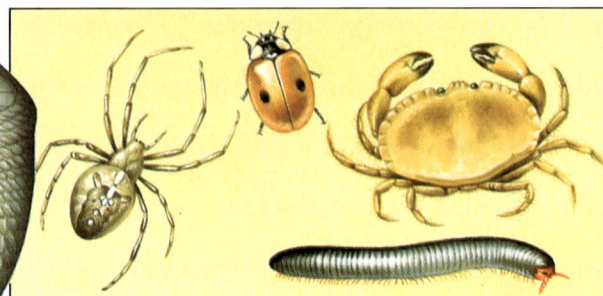

Q How do scientists know how many species exist?

A In 1982, biologist Terry Erwin found 163 new beetle species in one species of tropical rainforest tree. Using this information and what he already knew about different species, Erwin estimated that there were 100 million species in the world. It will be difficult to prove him right or wrong!

Between 1979 and 1988, 23,080 new species of beetle and 13,496 new species of spider were discovered.

Over 2307 new species of fish were discovered between 1979 and 1988.

Q How many new species are discovered every year?

A At present about 20,000 new species of animals are discovered every year. Species can be divided into different groups, such as insects. The pie chart below divides each year's new discoveries into these groups.

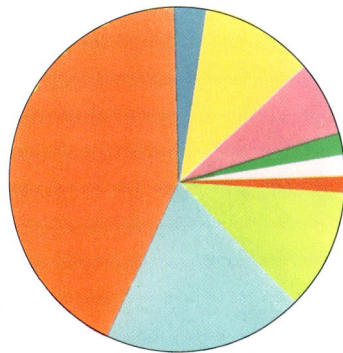

This pie chart is based on figures gathered between 1979 and 1988.

- Protozoa (single-celled animals)
- Soft-bodied invertebrates (worms and snails)
- Crustacea (eg. crabs)
- Other invertebrates (eg. jellyfish and starfish)
- Pisces (fish)
- Other chordata (amphibians and reptiles)
- Arachnida (spiders and scorpions)
- Coleoptera (beetles)
- All other insects

Q How long will it take us to find and describe every species?

A It has taken 250 years to find 1,700,000 species. If there *are* 100,000,000 species in all, it could take us at least another 14,000 years to find the rest. It may be impossible to find them all – ever!

Q Which types of new species are most likely to be undiscovered?

A Many new species of bacteria and fungi, which are small and often difficult to identify, are being discovered. In 1990, Norwegian researchers found over 4,000 new species of bacteria in a gram (less than a teaspoonful) of forest soil.

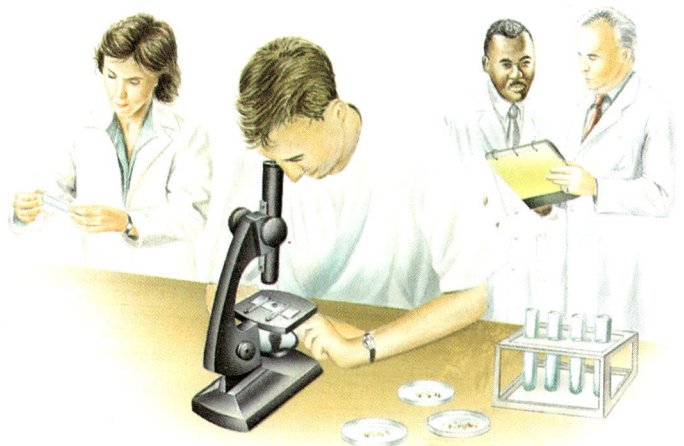

Q Have all viruses been discovered?

A New viruses – microscopic living organisms which cause diseases – are being discovered all the time. So far, 5,000 viruses have been discovered, but scientists think that as many as 500,000 may exist. The deadly Ebola virus that killed many people in Zaire in 1995 was only discovered in 1976.

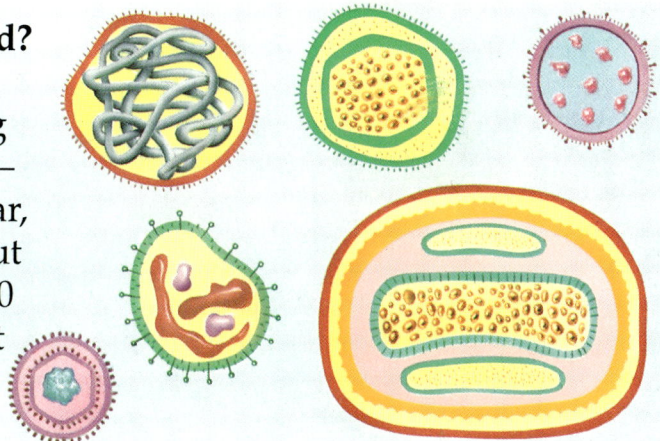

One square metre of woodland soil in Europe or North America can contain two million tiny animals, of up to 1,000 different species.

Where is there undiscovered life?

Most parts of Earth's surface have already been explored, but there are still many places where undiscovered life can be found. These are often remote and sometimes dangerous places.

Q Are there many undiscovered animals in the world's forests?

A Vast areas of forest, in Siberia and the rainforests of South America and South East Asia, have not been thoroughly explored. Scientists believe many undiscovered species must be hidden in them.

Q Will we find new species on mountains?

A High mountains in the tropics are often home to unique and new species. Roraima, a 2810 metre high mountain plateau rising above the Venezuelan rainforest, is home to many unusual species which live nowhere else.

Q Why are islands good places to look for new species?

A Islands almost always contain unique species which have evolved in different ways to their relatives on the mainland. In 1990, a new monkey – the black-faced lion tamarin – was found on the island of Superaqui, just 65 kilometres from the Brazilian city of São Paulo.

Q Have we discovered all the species that live in the seas?

A Scientific researchers constantly survey oceans, but every voyage still uncovers new species – some microscopic and some huge. The pygmy beaked whale was only discovered in 1991.

Detailed studies of kiwis in New Zealand have shown that there are four species of this flightless bird, not three as was once thought.

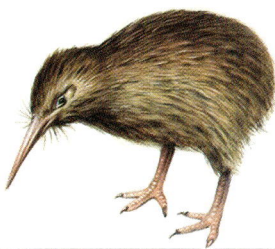

It has been estimated that half of the plants in the tropical rainforests of Columbia have not yet been described.

Q What other habitats are likely to be home to new species?

A The soil, caves and coral reefs still hide many species. Hot springs, where water bubbles to the surface from deep underground, cold polar seas and deserts all contain specialised forms of life that have not been described.

Q Will we find new life in deep lakes?

A Large freshwater lakes often contain unique species. Lake Malawi in Africa contains 500 species of fish that are found nowhere else on Earth. Fish experts – ichthiologists – estimate that less than half of the different types of fish in Lake Malawi have been found so far.

Q If living things are studied more closely, will we find more species?

A As scientists discover more about life, they often find that what they thought was one species may really be two or more. Until recently it was thought that there was only one type of pipistrelle bat in Britain, but some scientists now believe that there may be two, because they have found that there are two types with different squeaks.

Q Is there life on the seabed?

A Until about 125 years ago most biologists did not believe that there was any life in the deep ocean. Between 1872 and 1876, biologists aboard the research ship *HMS Challenger* found many new animals at great depths. Since then, many expeditions have found new species of fish, jellyfish, squid, worms, clams and crabs living thousands of metres below the surface.

Collections of seeds are often stored at low temperatures in seed banks, where some species will survive for hundreds of years.

Who makes new discoveries?

Although zoologists and biologists discover animals and plants, explorers are also well-known for bringing back unknown animals and creatures from their travels.

Q Can searching for new species be dangerous?

A Collecting new species has always been difficult and dangerous. The famous Scottish plant collector David Douglas was killed by a wild bull in Hawaii in 1834, whilst collecting new plants for European gardeners to grow. Today's collectors often travel to deserts, polar regions, high mountains or under the sea. Hazards can range from sandstorms, blizzards, extreme temperatures, avalanches and landslides to poisonous snakes and scorpions, tropical diseases and sharks.

Alpine poppy

Q How do explorers search for new plants and animals?

A Zoos, botanic gardens and natural history museums send expeditions all over the world. Small, well organised teams of skilled biologists use modern technology, like light aircraft, satellite navigation aids and computers, but these expeditions into remote places are often still dangerous.

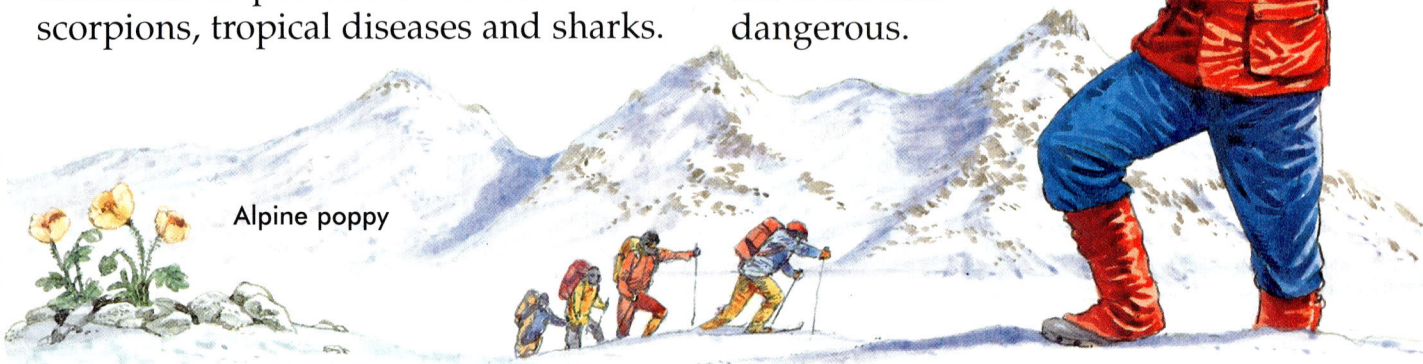

Q How do zoos help in discovering new species?

A Captured examples of new animal species are often sent to zoos, where they can be examined by experts, who study details of the animals and their behaviour. Zoos are safe places where rare animals can breed. When their numbers increase, they can often be released back into the wild.

The herbarium at Kew Gardens, in London, contains 6 million pressed plant species.

Over 30,000 different plants (about 10% of all known species) are grown at Kew Gardens.

Q Have explorers discovered any new foods?

A Famous explorer Christopher Columbus brought chilli peppers back from North America. Other edible discoveries include the potato and cacao (for making chocolate), which were both discovered by the Spanish Conquistadors in South America.

Q What are botanic gardens for?

A Collections of important living plants are grown and studied in botanic gardens. They often contain a plant library called an herbarium. The first specimen of every new plant discovered is usually photographed, described, pressed and stored in an herbarium.

Q What do natural history museums contain?

A Natural history museums store millions of photographs and specimens of plants and skins, eggs and skeletons of animal species. They display some of their collections, to teach people about the importance of understanding the natural world.

Q What happens to new species?

A As most new species cannot be identifed immediately, specimens are sent to natural history museums, where experts compare them with known species.

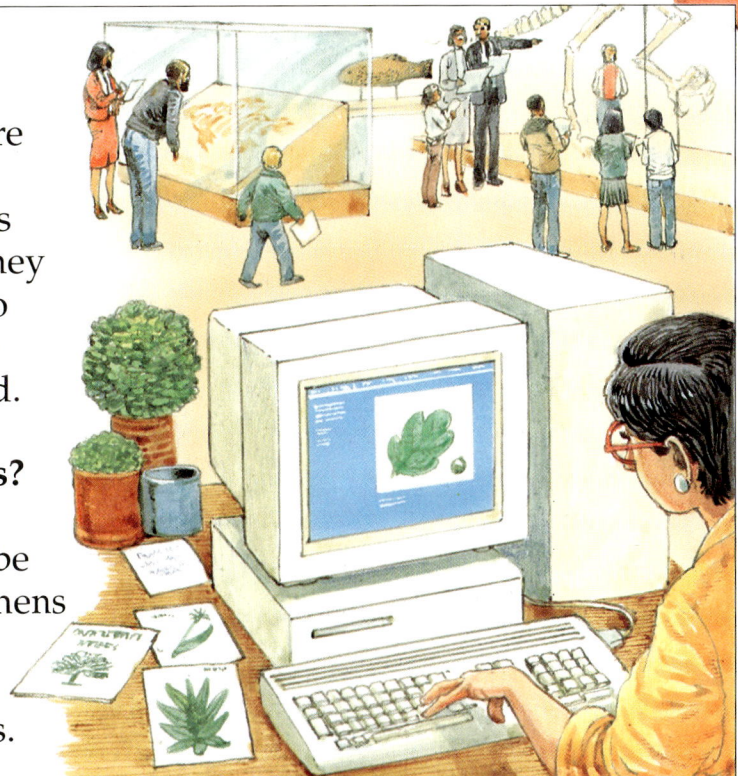

The kouprey, a two metre-tall wild grey ox from Cambodia, was first seen by scientists in 1936. Only about 400 koupreys survive today.

Are there recent discoveries?

S ome large and spectacular animals have been discovered in the 20th century. Even big animals can remain undiscovered in remote places.

Q Have any monsters been discovered in the 20th century?

A At the beginning of the 20th century, scientists investigated reports of fierce dragons living on the small, volcanic island of Komodo in Indonesia. They discovered the Komodo dragon, which is the world's largest lizard, at over 3 metres long. It can kill pigs and deer and has been known to eat people.

Q Have any more unusual animals been discovered recently?

A One of the most important finds was the okapi, a short-necked giraffe that lives in dense jungle in the Congo and Zaïre. This strange animal, part zebra, part giraffe, was first spotted in 1909, although skins and skeletons had been found earlier.

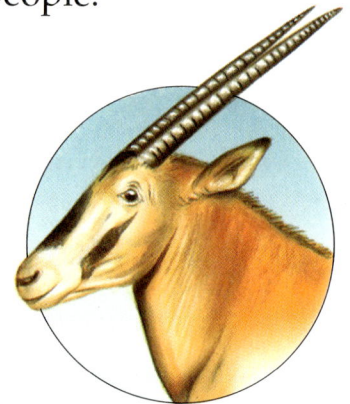

Q Are new large mammals still being found today?

A In 1992 John MacKinnon of the World Wide Fund for Nature described the first specimen of the Vu Quang ox, a horned animal as big as a goat, that lives in the remote forests of Vietnam. Only one Vu Quang ox has been captured alive.

The world's largest frog, the Goliath frog which weighs up to 3.5 kg, was only described in 1906.

In 1984 a fish specialist called Dr. Peter Henderson discovered a small, bright red blind catfish that lives on land. The fish lives in leaf litter beside rivers near Manaus in Brazil.

Q What is the most unusual modern wildlife discovery?

A The gastric-brooding frog, found in Southern Queensland, Australia in 1973 was very unusual indeed. A female swallows her eggs, which then hatch in her stomach. She spits out the tadpoles when they are old enough to fend for themselves. Sadly, the original wild colony of gastric-brooding frogs and all captive individuals have died out. Unless someone can find another colony, gastric-brooding frogs must now be considered extinct.

The Australian gastric-brooding frog

Q Are any 20th-century discoveries in pet shops?

A The neon tetra, discovered in 1936, is now one of the world's most popular aquarium fish. Millions of this colourful little fish are sold every year.

Q Are any recent animal discoveries kept as pets?

A Golden hamsters were discovered in 1879 but died out by 1910. Then, in 1930, Professor Israel Aharoni found a female and eleven young in a deep burrow near Aleppo in Syria. All golden hamsters in pet shops around the world are descended from just three of the animals that Aharoni found!

Q What is the most unusual rediscovery of the 20th century?

A The Takahe – a kind of moorhen – was discovered on South Island, New Zealand in 1849, but the species was officially declared extinct at the end of the 19th century. But in 1948, around remote Lake Te Anau, a thriving Takahe colony was discovered.

Q What is the most gruesome new discovery?

A In 1994, biologists in Brazil found a new kind of vampire fish that is only 1 cm long. It feeds on the blood of other fish, but can wriggle into the bodies of swimmers in the Amazon river, to drink their blood.

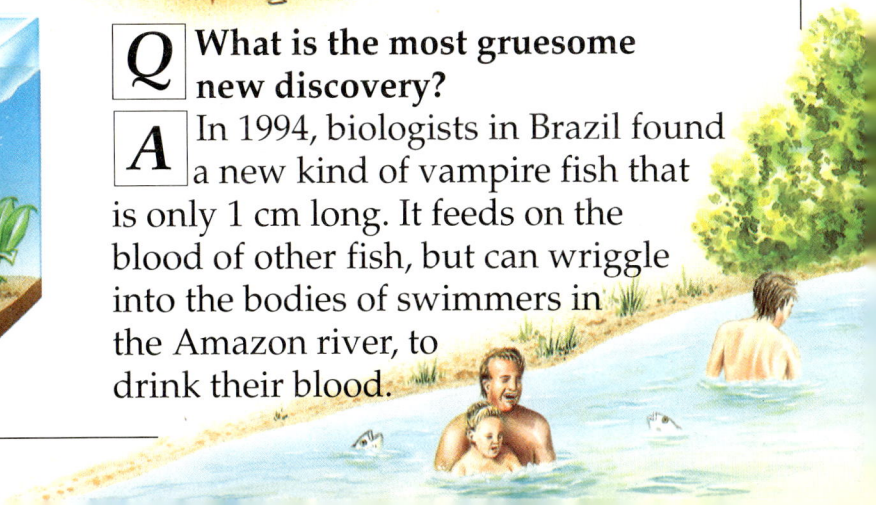

New life on the ocean floor is often collected by scooping it up with deep dredges or surveyed with remote-controlled TV cameras.

Is there new life on the ocean floor?

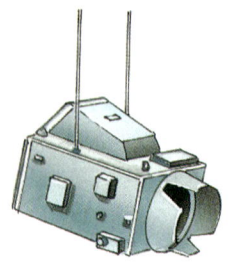

Although the oceans cover 71 per cent of the surface of the Earth, the sea is the least explored part of our planet. Plankton floats on the surface and life can be found at great depths.

Q Have there been any exciting discoveries in the oceans recently?

A In 1994, a team of scientists discovered a new carnivorous sponge in the Mediterranean Sea. Sponges usually filter tiny food particles from water, but this one catches and kills shrimps.

Q How can sea creatures help us?

A Recently, scientists have discovered several useful medicines in sea creatures that can help cure human illnesses and diseases. Strange sea animals called sea squirts contain a chemical called Didemnin B, which can be used to treat cancer. Dogfish contain a new kind of antibiotic called squalamine, which kills bacteria.

Dogfish

Q Where have the most unusual new discoveries been made?

A In 1977, scientists discovered completely new types of animals living over 2,500 metres below the ocean surface, around thermal vents. Thermal vents are undersea volcanoes that belch fire, smoke and poisonous chemicals.

Most deep-sea animals, like the painted lobster, feed on dead animals that fall on to the sea bed.

Vestimentiferans have no gut. They depend completely on the bacteria in their bodies to supply them with food.

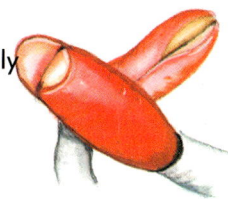

Deep-sea submersible

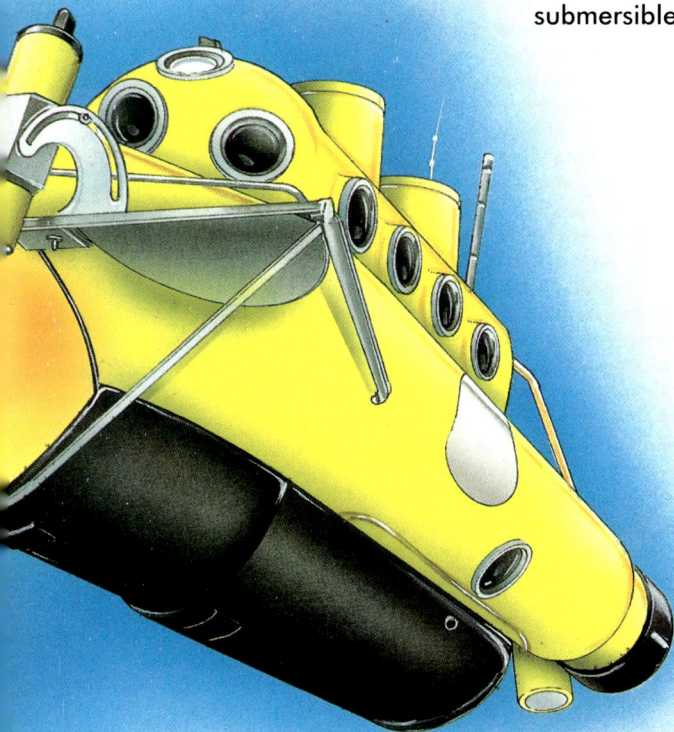

Q **How do thermal vent animals survive?**

A They live in darkness, so there are no plants for them to feed on. Plants cannot survive in the dark depths of the sea as they can only exist in light. Instead thermal vent animals contain mysterious bacteria that use sulphur from the thermal vents to make energy.

Q **How do biologists explore dangerous thermal vents?**

A Biologists use special, strengthened miniature submarines, called deep-sea submersibles, which can dive to over 3,000 metres. These are equipped with lights and television cameras that relay pictures to the surface. Specimens are collected with remote-control robot arms operated by the scientists from the safety of the submersible.

Q **How do deep-sea animals adapt to life on the sea bed?**

A Many deep-sea animals have odd features that allow them to adapt to their surroundings. One example is the strange tripod fish, which can live at depths of almost 8,000 metres. It has a long, thin tail and fins, so that it can sit on the sea bottom like a tripod.

Q **What kinds of animals live around thermal vents?**

A Large clams, blind white crabs and giant tube worms called Riftia live around thermal vents. The giant tube worms are so different from any other form of life that scientists invented a completely new name for them – Vestimentiferans. This name means "to wear a garment" and was given to the creatures because they live inside hard tubes.

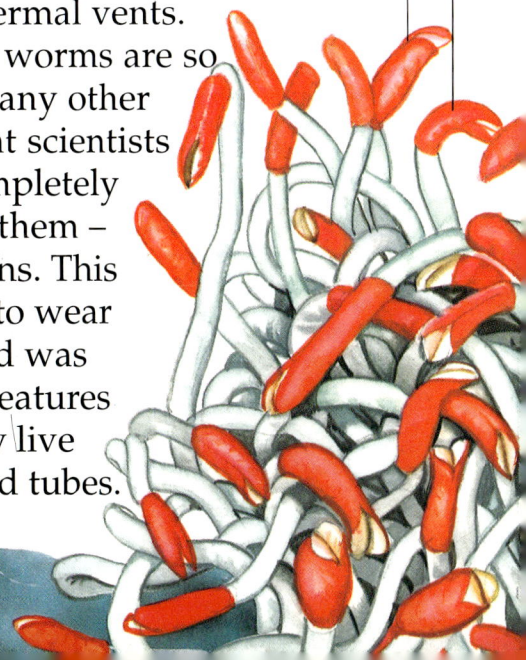

The Kraken of Norse mythology, which created whirlpools and sank ships, was probably a giant squid.

Are there really sea monsters?

Most early explorers brought back frightening stories of sea monsters that they saw on their voyages. No real monsters have ever been discovered, but large animals could easily live in the sea without being seen.

Q Are there very large sea creatures still undiscovered in the oceans?

A The megamouth shark, which is over 5 metres long, was only discovered in 1976 when a dead specimen was washed up on a beach. Since the first living specimen was filmed in 1990, only a few specimens have been found, despite constant searches.

Megamouth shark

Q Could there be monster animals in the ocean depths?

A Monster giant squid, which may reach a length of over 10 metres, are very rarely seen on the surface. Most live in very deep water, and are only found when dead specimens are washed up on the shore.

Giant squid

Q Do any monster-like animals lurk in the sea?

A Some of the ugliest animals on Earth live in the ocean depths. Deep-sea hatchet fish, angler fish and gulpers have long needle-shaped teeth and glow in the dark. They may not be very large, but they certainly look like monsters.

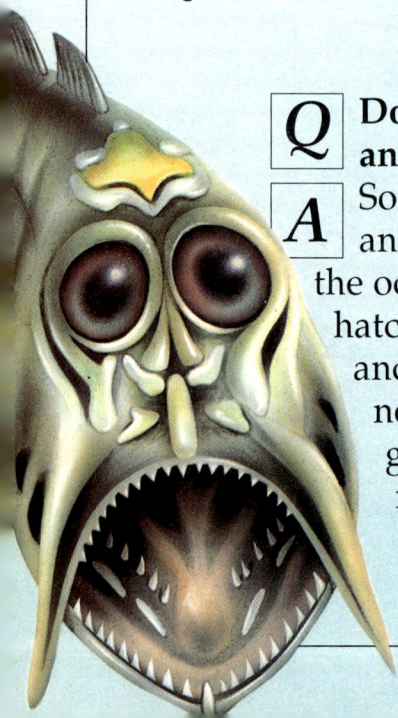

Q Are there undiscovered mammals in the sea?

A Several species of large dolphins and beaked whales have only been spotted a few times. Hector's beaked whale and Longman's beaked whale are only known from skulls washed up on beaches. There could easily be more undiscovered mammals in the oceans.

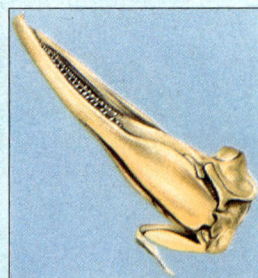

A completely new kind of parasitic tapeworm was discovered in the gut of the first megamouth shark when it was dissected.

Eleven species of whale have been discovered in the last 80 years.

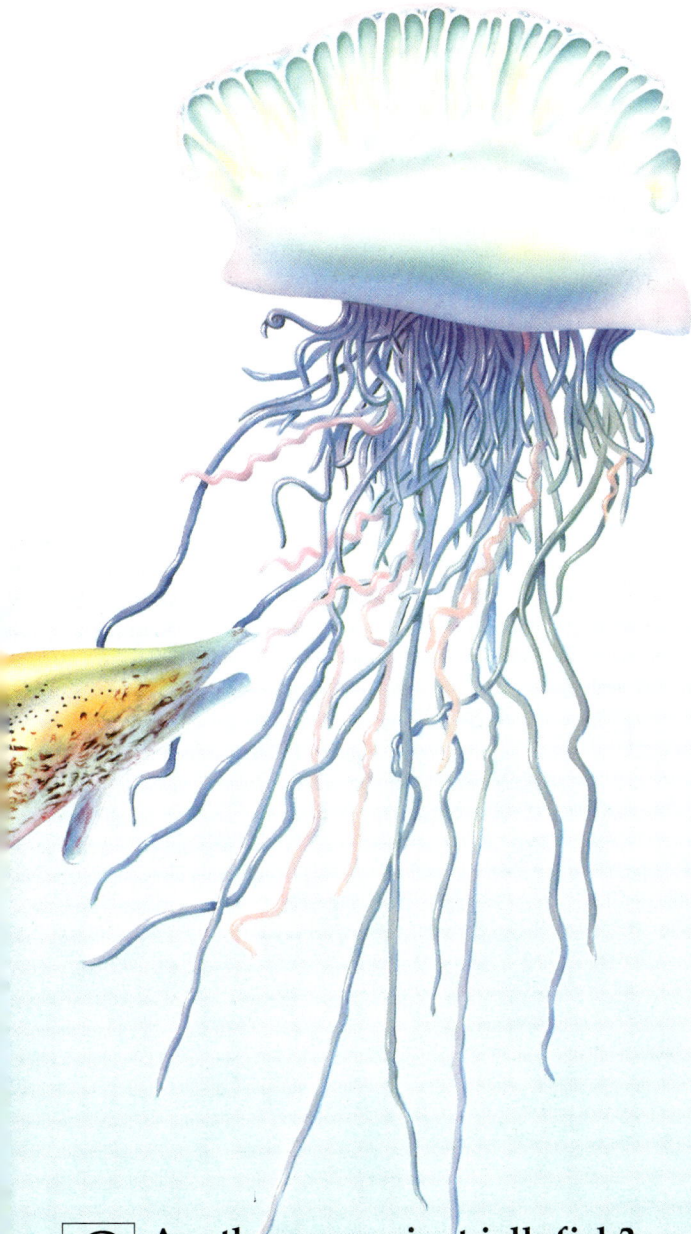

Q Did sailors really see mermaids?

A Some biologists believe that sailors may have mistaken sunbathing seals or sea mammals called manatees for humans. Explorers on long voyages often suffered from fevers and delirium, caused by diseases like scurvy. They may have imagined they saw mermaids instead of animals.

Q How can sailors' reports of sea monsters be explained?

A Sailors may have seen dead, floating deep-sea animals. These animals live under enormous pressures at great depths and as they float to the surface they can inflate, as the sea's pressure decreases. The deep-sea oarfish has a head like a horse, and a long red mane. Its ribbon-shaped body is over 9 metres long. When it floats to the surface it looks like old pictures of sea monsters.

Q Are there any giant jellyfish?

A The poisonous lion's mane jellyfish is usually only about half a metre across, but giant specimens that are 2 metres in diameter have been found in the Arctic Ocean. The stinging tentacles of the Portuguese Man-o'-War jellyfish can be over 10 metres long and even larger jellyfish-like creatures have been sighted in the deep oceans.

Although a Sasquatch has been filmed, many people believe the film to be a hoax.

Do mythical monsters exist?

There are frequent reports of large unidentified animals from many parts of the world, including Loch Ness in Scotland and the Himalayan mountain range. People have tried for many years to collect scientific evidence that these animals exist.

Q Is there a Loch Ness monster?

A There are films and photographs of monster-shaped objects that appear to be swimming in Loch Ness. Some people believe that animals like the plesiosaurs, which died out 65 million years ago, might live there. Numerous scientific expeditions have failed to prove that the monster exists.

Q Have other monsters been spotted around the world?

A Early explorers in Central Africa brought back tales of an animal with an elephant-like body, a long neck, a small head and large claws. This description resembles a small sauropod dinosaur. A Congolese scientist claimed to have seen it in 1983, but few people outside Africa believe that it exists.

Q Do apemen exist?

A Gorilla-like animals which walk on their hind legs have been sighted in North America, the Himalayas, China and Mongolia. However, no apeman – or apewoman – has ever been captured.

Q If apemen do exist, where are they most likely to be found?

A There have been thousands of reported sightings of apes about 2 metres tall (taller than most humans), in the forests of Western North America. This mysterious creature has been named Sasquatch, or Bigfoot (because of the huge footprints which have been found). Some zoologists believe they could be the last surviving giant apes that became extinct in China 300,000 years ago.

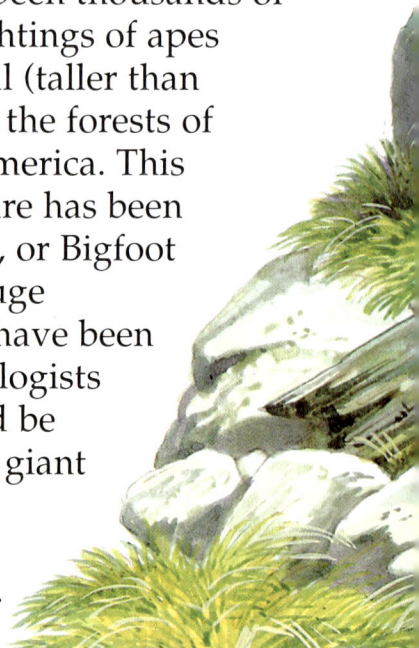

Sir Peter Scott, the famous naturalist, gave the Loch Ness monster the scientific name Nessiteras rhombopteryx, which means 'Ness Monster with a diamond-shaped fin.'

When the letters are rearranged these words are also an anagram of 'Monster hoax by Sir Peter S.'

Q Have other apemen been seen?

A There have been reports of apes called Almas from the Pamir mountains of Asia. Almas are said to look like Neanderthals – early humans supposed to have died out 35,000 years ago.

Q Have apemen been reported recently?

A In 1994, Debbie Martyr, a journalist travelling through the forests of Sumatra, saw a short ape walking upright. Local people call the animal an orang pendek and say that it is strong enough to uproot small trees. Debbie Martyr has returned to Sumatra, to try to photograph the animal.

Q Is there an abominable snowman?

A A few climbers have found large footprints in the Himalayan snow. Some people claimed that they were made by the Yeti, or abominable snowman.

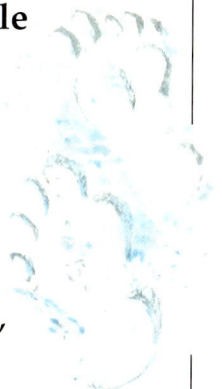

In 1985, giant red fish, estimated to be 10 metres long, were sighted in Lake Hanas in Northwest China. As yet, none has been captured.

Do large undiscovered animals exist?

Large parts of Australia, Asia and even North America are still sparsely populated and have not been properly studied by scientists. There are many places where large animals may remain undiscovered.

Q Have any 'extinct' animals ever been found?

A Australian flightless night parrots were believed to have become extinct in 1912, but a dead specimen was found on a road in 1990. It is possible the parrot might still exist.

Australian flightless night parrot

Q If a species has been discovered, is it easy to find more specimens?

A No, not necessarily. The taipan, one of Australia's most venomous snakes, was discovered in dense forests in Queensland in 1867, but another specimen was not collected until 1923. Shy animals can remain hidden for a long time.

Q Is it true that some prehistoric animals might still exist?

A Scientists once believed that all mammoths died out at least 12,000 years ago. However, in 1993, Russian scientists discovered remains of mammoths that died only 4,000 years ago. The discovery on remote Wrangle Island in the Arctic Ocean has led to speculation that mammoths might still live in some uninhabited parts of Siberia.

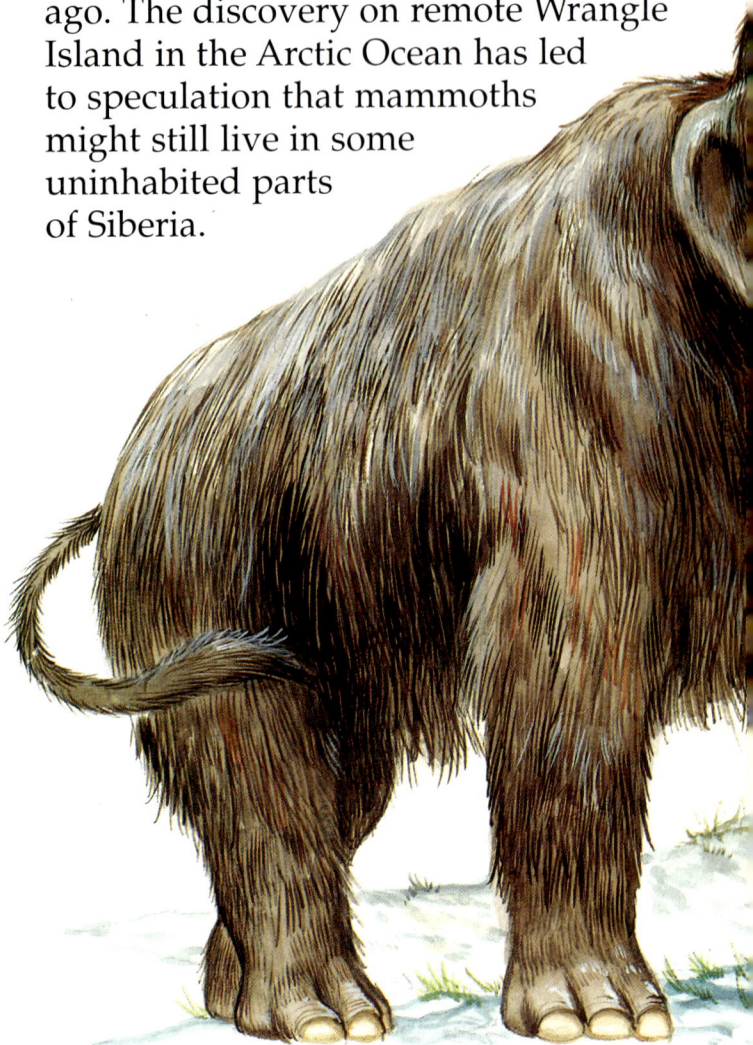

A species of giant earwig which lives on the island of St. Helena has not been seen since 1965, despite several attempts to find it again. It spends most of its life underground, so it may still exist.

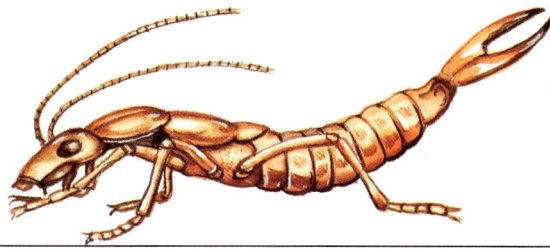

Mammoths died out at around the same time the ancient Egyptians were building the pyramids.

Q Have other 'extinct' birds been rediscovered?

A Ivory-billed woodpeckers, which were thought to have become extinct in North America in the 1930s, were discovered again 30 years later. Ornithologists believe that a few of these spectacular woodpeckers may still exist in the United States.

Q Can animals remain hidden because they are so rare?

A Thylacines, or Tasmanian wolves, became extinct in 1936 but many people believe that a few rare survivors still exist. Footprints have been found and some people claim to have seen thylacines, but a living specimen has not been captured since 1936.

Q Could large animals remain hidden in Britain?

A Many people claim to have seen large cats roaming the countryside. These are thought to be escaped pet pumas or large cats. They sometimes eat sheep, but no one has yet caught or shot one of these elusive beasts.

The maidenhair tree (Ginkgo biloba) is a living fossil that still survives. The fan-shaped leaves of its relatives are found as fossils in rocks.

What are 'living fossils'?

We only know that dinosaurs existed because we find their fossil bones. Sometimes we uncover rare living examples of ancient groups of plants and animals that we thought had died long ago. We call these 'living fossils'.

Q What is the most famous living fossil?

A The coelacanth, is a primitive ancestor of the first animals with backbones to invade land. Coelacanths were once only known as fossils in 380 million year-old rocks. They were thought to have died out 65 million years ago, until a living specimen was discovered in 1938. A small colony lives in caves off the Comoro Islands in the Indian ocean.

Coelacanth

Tuatara

Q What can living fossils tell us about the history of life on Earth?

A Living fossils can tell us how the ancestors of modern organisms lived. For example, in 1952, a shellfish called Neopilina, thought to have been extinct for 350 million years, was dredged up from the seabed off the Mexican coast. The Neopilina is different from modern molluscs and can tell us a great deal about its ancient ancestors.

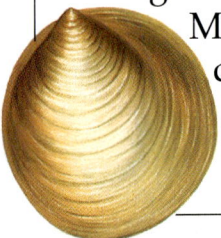

Q Are there living fossil dinosaurs?

A The tuatara from New Zealand is a lizard-like reptile, which closely resembles early ancestors of dinosaurs. Tuatara fossils have been found in 200 million year-old rocks. Somehow it has survived, although the dinosaurs that evolved from its extinct relatives died out 65 million years ago.

South American hoatzins have some of the characteristics of extinct pterosaurs, that died out 65 million years ago. Like pterosaurs, young hoatzins have claws on their wings, that help them to scramble through tree tops.

Q Are there living fossil plants?

A The Dawn redwood, discovered in China in 1945, is the last surviving species of a kind of tree that was common 100 million years ago.

Q Are there any common living fossils that we can see today?

A Modern plants called horsetails are smaller versions of giant horsetails that lived 300 million years ago. Only 29 horsetail species survive, although they once formed dense forests of 30 metre-tall trees. Horsetails are common garden weeds and are also found around pond edges, in similar habitats to the swamps that their ancestors grew in.

Q Can living fossils provide us with anything useful?

A Horseshoe crabs, found on the sea bed, are living fossil relatives of the trilobites which died out 250 million years ago. Horseshoe crabs have blue blood, which can be used by doctors to detect dangerous bacteria, such as those that cause meningitis in children.

Q Will we find any more living fossils?

A Almost certainly. Another 40 metre-tall tree, the Wollemi pine, was discovered in a remote gorge in Australia in 1994. Wollemi pines are survivors of an ancient group of pines that died out 80 million years ago. They are related to present-day Monkey puzzle trees.

The last brown bears in Britain were probably killed in the 8th century.

When the last individual of a species dies, that species becomes extinct. It is gone for ever and can never return. In the past, natural disasters often led to extinction of species, but today they mostly disappear because of human interference.

Q What were mass extinctions?

A Millions of years ago, many terrible natural disasters occurred on Earth. These may have been caused by changes of climate, like ice ages, or by collisions with asteroids from outer space. Climates altered, sea levels rose or fell and thousands of species died out in very short periods of time.

Q Are human activities causing mass extinctions?

A The destruction of tropical forests and the pollution of land, sea and air is destroying hundreds of species every year.

Q What may have caused the mass extinction of the dinosaurs?

A Many geologists believe that a massive asteroid collided with Earth. Huge clouds of dust were thrown into the air, the climate changed and all the dinosaurs died.

Q Why did all dinosaurs die, but other animals and plants survive?

A No one is really sure. The change in climate may not have suited the dinosaurs but other animals, such as birds and mammals, may have been able to survive better under the new conditions.

The flightless great auk was tame and easy for people to catch, so sailors killed thousands for food and oil. The last great auk was killed in Iceland in 1844.

The last British wolf was killed in Scotland in 1743.

Q What well-known plants are in danger of extinction?

A Although millions of African violets are grown as house plants every year, they are in danger of extinction in their wild habitat.

African violet

Q Why do flightless birds like dodos become extinct so easily?

Dodo

A These birds often lost the power of flight because they evolved on islands where they had no enemies and therefore no fear of people or predators. These trusting flightless birds were easily killed. One such example is the dodo which lived on the island of Mauritius. Dodos were either hunted for food or killed by the rats and pigs brought by explorers – the species was extinct only 150 years after it was first discovered.

Q Which other birds have been wiped out by hunting?

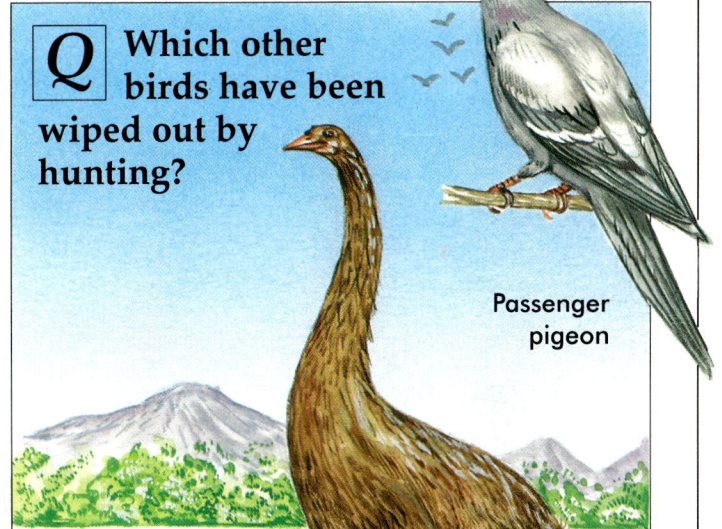

Passenger pigeon

New Zealand moa

A The moa, a massive flightless bird like an ostrich, was wiped out by Maori hunters in New Zealand before the first Europeans arrived there. Passenger pigeons, which once gathered in flocks of millions of birds that stretched for 32 kilometres or more, were completely wiped out in North America by 1914.

The breeds of dog which people keep as pets are all one species, but each breed has different mutations.

Are new species evolving?

Even though many species are disappearing, new ones are formed all the time. New species survive because they are better suited to their surroundings than an old species.

Q What is evolution?

A Evolution is the process where species change as time goes by. Small changes occur all the time in species and sometimes they allow them to live in places where the original, unchanged species could not survive. If the new species can survive better than the original one, it increases and may replace the old one.

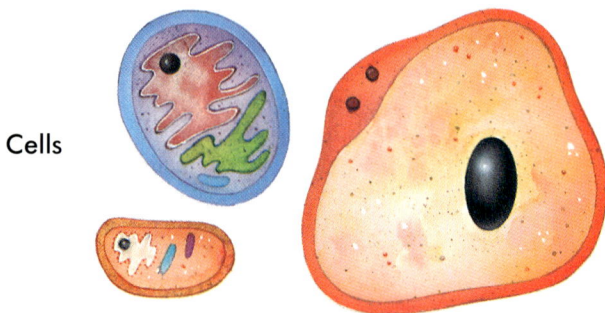

Cells

Look out for white blackbirds and squirrels, whose cells have mutated so that their feathers and fur are white. Mutations like these are called albinos.

Q How does evolution occur?

A All living things are made up of cells, which, in turn, contain genes. These form a code containing all the instructions needed to make a new copy of a plant or animal. When eggs or seeds are produced, a small part of this code can suddenly change, or mutate. This mutation alters the appearance of its owner.

Q Can we see evolution happening?

A The first signs of evolution are often the appearance of new forms of a species with small changes, such as different colours of flowers and insects. Some ladybirds have evolved new wing case colours, so they have red spots on black wing cases instead of the reverse.

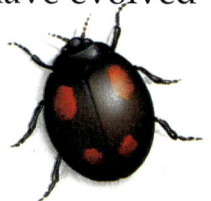

Radioactivity can cause mutations. Scientists sometimes expose plants to radioactivity when they want to produce crops with new mutations, like dwarfness.

Q Do all organisms with mutations become new species?

A No. Many mutations are harmful to their owners. White blackbirds, for example, are easily spotted and caught by cats, so they do not usually survive long enough to lay eggs. But if conditions were to change (if it were to snow for a long time), white black birds would be harder to spot and would survive better. Then they might replace black blackbirds.

Mutations allow living things to adapt to a changing environment.

Q How fast do new species evolve?

A Big changes, like the evolution of wings or legs, have taken millions of years, but small changes can happen quite quickly. New forms of moths called melanics, with dark wings instead of pale ones, evolved in some cities in the space of a few years. The dark forms are harder for birds to see on sooty walls and tree trunks, so they survive better and quickly increase, while the pale ones are found by birds and eaten.

Many garden roses have been created by crossing a rose from China, called Rosa chinesis, with species from other parts of the world.

Q Can scientists create new species?

A Scientists have often created new plant species by crossing species that already exist. For example, by crossing wheat and rye, scientists have created a new cereal called Triticale.

Q What types of living things evolve fastest?

A Organisms like viruses, bacteria, fungi and insects evolve fastest. Because they multiply quickly and exist in enormous numbers, there is a bigger chance that mutations will happen and the organism will evolve.

Drugs that may help in the treatment of viruses have been discovered in daisies and an Australian plant called Moreton Bay Chestnut.

Can we find threatened species?

Every year, thousands of species of animals and plants become extinct because their habitats are being destroyed. We are unlikely to find them all before they disappear forever.

Q Do many types of living organism become extinct every day?

A Some scientists estimate that about three species become extinct every hour. If this is true, over seventy species become extinct every day.

Q Does it matter if some species become extinct?

A It is important to look after the living world and take care of all the other creatures that share our planet, but there are also practical reasons why we should protect species. A plant that becomes extinct today might contain a medicine that could have saved lives tomorrow.

Q How can we find new species before they become extinct?

A The best way to stop extinctions is to protect natural habitats and prevent the pollution of the air, land and water. We also need to train more scientists to find and identify species.

Q What kind of medicines occur in plants?

A Some plants contain drugs that can cure serious diseases. Madagascan periwinkle, for example, contains drugs called vincristine and vinblastin which cure some forms of cancer in children.

These drugs are worth about US$200 million per year.

Q Do everyday medicines come from plants?

A Almost half of the medicines that you can buy in a chemist without a doctor's prescription contain drugs from plants. Aspirin, a commonly-used painkiller, was first discovered in willow twigs, although it is now produced artificially in laboratories.

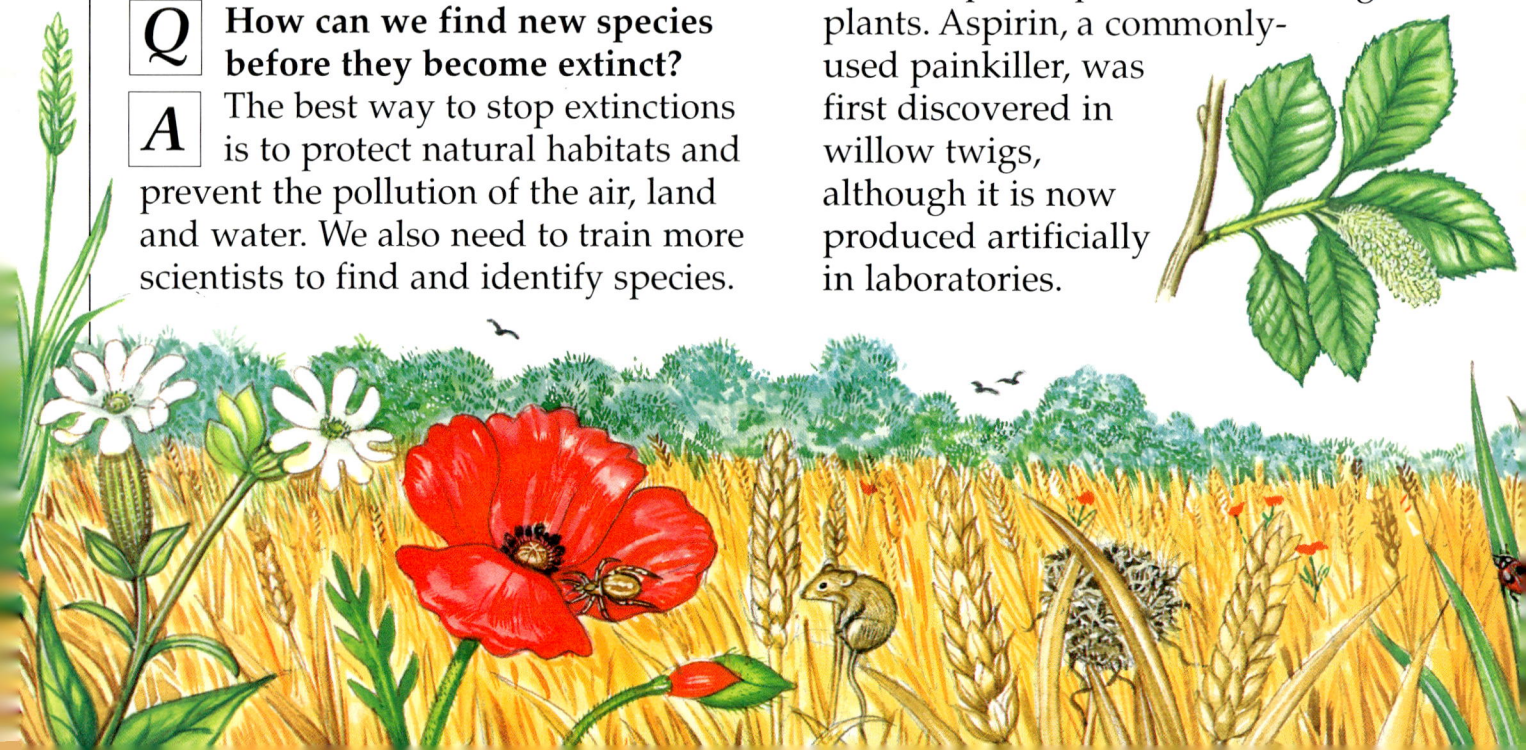

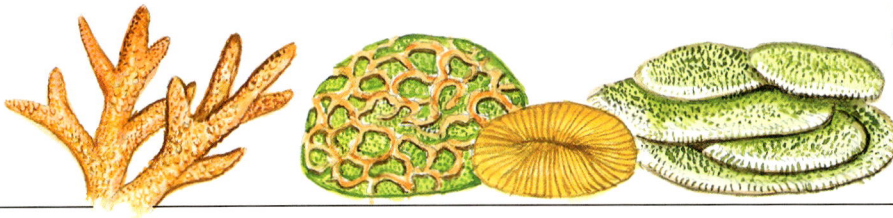

Doctors have used pieces of coral to make artificial eyes that move naturally. Blood vessels grow in the coral's tiny pores, then new tissue joins the artificial eye to the eye muscles.

Q How was penicillin discovered?

A The antibiotic penicillin, which cures infections from bacteria, was accidentally discovered in mould (a type of fungus) by British scientist Alexander Fleming. A speck of mould fell on to a sample of the bacteria which causes blood poisoning. Fleming later noticed that the bacteria around the mould had been killed.

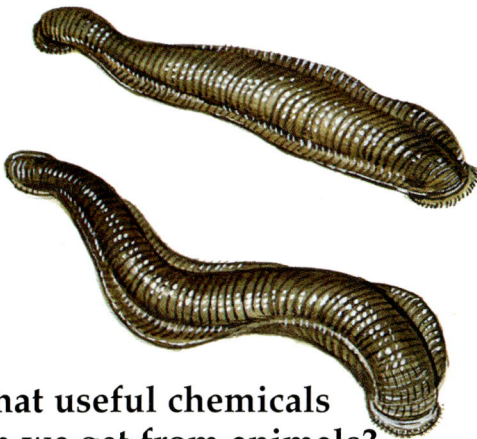

Q What useful chemicals can we get from animals?

A Medicinal leeches contain hirudin, a compound which stops blood from clotting. Hirudin is used to stop dangerous blood clots forming in people who have had hospital operations. Medicinal leeches are now becoming quite rare.

Q Can we deep-freeze species that are about to become extinct?

A Eggs of animals and seeds and buds of plants can be stored for many years if they are frozen in liquid nitrogen, at a temperature of -196°C. Sometimes they can be thawed out and brought back to life. The science of freezing living things is called cryogenics. It may be one way of saving endangered species.

North American condors and African vultures look similar, but scientists have compared their DNA to show that they aren't closely related.

Can we recreate dinosaurs?

In the movie 'Jurassic Park', scientists recreated dinosaurs by adding DNA from extinct dinosaurs to the eggs of frogs. This was just science fiction - an exciting story - but scientists can now change living things by altering their DNA, in a process called genetic engineering.

Q What is DNA?

A All the information for making a living organism is contained in its genes - a kind of chemical code - inside its cells. Genes are made from a chemical called deoxyribonucleic acid, or DNA. Living things evolve when their DNA code changes, producing mutations.

Q Can scientists understand and alter the code inside cells?

A DNA can be extracted and the code that it contains can be read. Scientists can now change the code, or move bits of it between different plants and animals. This is genetic engineering.

Q Can the genetic code be extracted from dead animals?

A Scientists have extracted pieces of DNA from the bones of animals that became extinct thousands of years ago. This ancient DNA can tell us how today's plants are different from their ancient and extinct ancestors.

Q What useful things can we do with genetic engineering?

A Genetic engineering allows us to put useful genes into crops to protect them from pests. For example, anti-freeze genes from fish that live in the Antarctic could be put into plants, to protect them from frost. This is another reason why it is so important to find and protect unknown species.

Condors are more closely related to storks - they just look like vultures because they have evolved to survive in similar environments.

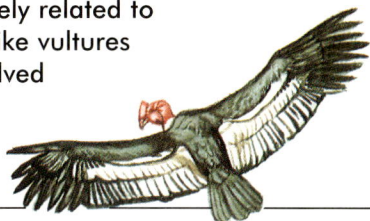

Some animals, such as fireflies, glow in the dark. Genetic engineers can put firefly genes into plants, so they can glow in the dark too!

Q Could we recreate giant birds, like the extinct moas of New Zealand?

A It might be possible. Genetic engineers have recently transferred genes from other animals to mice and fish, making them grow much larger and faster than normal. By this method salmon have been genetically engineered to grow over ten times larger than normal. If the same technique worked on ostriches, they might grow as large as moas!

Q Can we use DNA to help us to recreate extinct species?

A It may be possible. Quaggas are extinct relatives of zebras. Samples of DNA from quagga skins in museums are almost the same as today's zebra DNA. If we find zebras whose DNA is similar to quagga DNA, we may be able to breed herds of animals that look more like quaggas than zebras.

Q Can frozen plants be grown again?

A Frozen plant specimens are stored for many years and can be thawed out and grown again if they are needed. The Mexican hot chocolate flower (which smells of chocolate) is probably extinct in the wild, but deep-frozen material from cultivated plants is stored at Kew Gardens. Botanists are planning to reintroduce this plant to its original habitat.

Q Can we store genes if the plants and animals they came from are dead?

A DNA from many sorts of living things can be cut into small sections and inserted in bacteria, which then grow in nutrient jelly with these extra genes inside them. Thousands of different genes can be stored in bacteria colonies for future use.

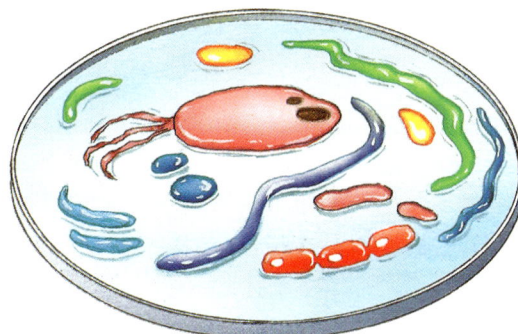

Ask for a microscope as a present. It will allow you to explore a hidden world of tiny animals and plants.

How can you make new discoveries?

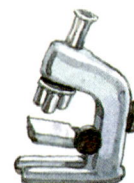

There are still plenty of opportunities to discover new species and to learn more about those that have already been found. The best way to do this is to become a biologist.

Q How can I become a biologist?

A Start in your own backyard, by learning about plants and animals that live around you. Learn to identify different types of living things.

Q Should I make collections of plants and animals?

A The best way to study wildlife is not to collect and kill it, but to watch the ways in which plants and animals live. Draw and describe what you see, so that you can identify your discoveries later with the help of books. Learn to use cameras and camcorders to record the living things around you. If you study them you may make new discoveries about the ways that they live.

Q Are there any organisations that can help me?

A Join your local natural history society, which will probably organise field meetings in the summer, so that you can search for rare animals and plants in your area. Conservation societies and wildlife trusts are also full of people who can help you to learn about the natural world.

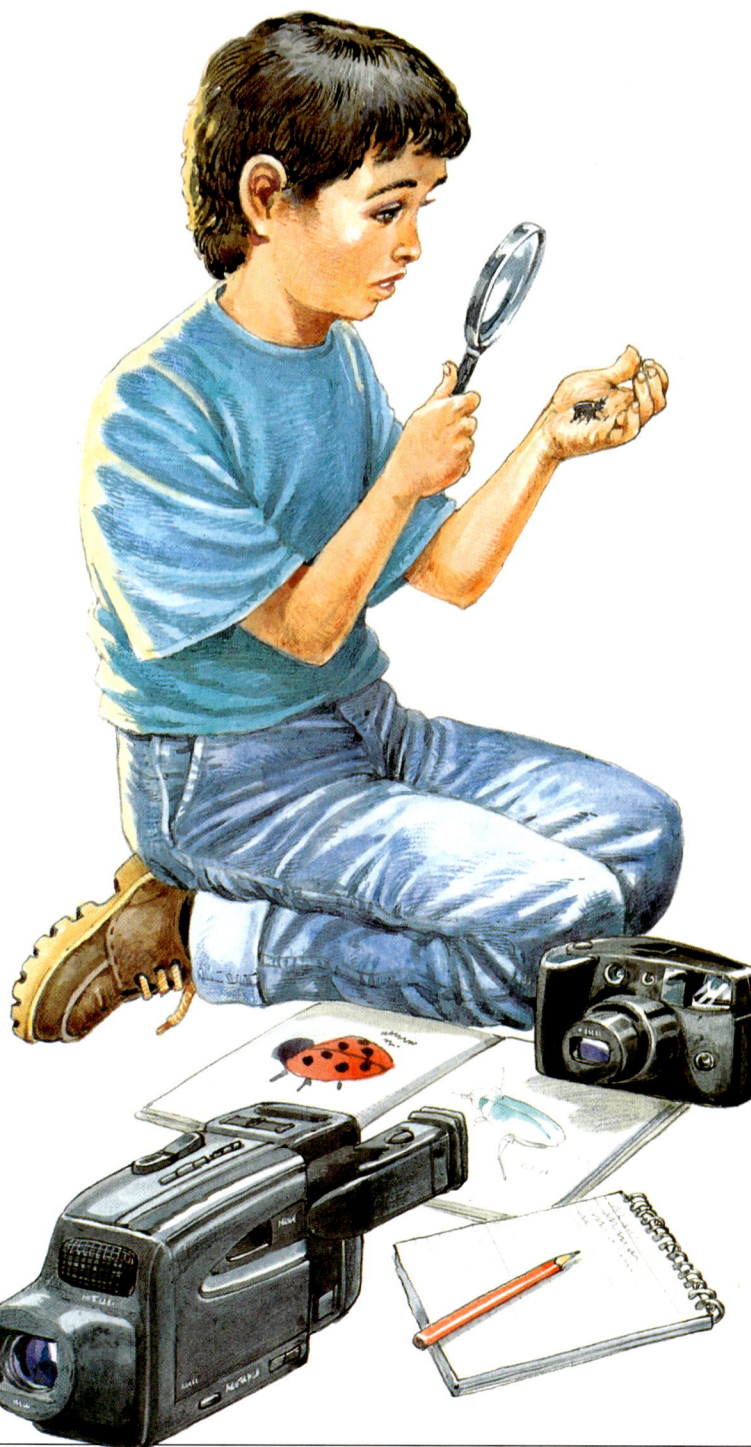

The plant Berberis darwinii is named after Charles Darwin. He also has a frog named after him.

Your local library or museum can give you information about local natural history societies.

Q Could a new species be named after me?

A It is possible, if you become a famous biologist. There are plenty of organisms that still need names! Charles Darwin, who first proved that living things can evolve, has several plants named after him.

Q How can I help to save species now?

A By helping to support the work of organisations like the World Wide Fund for Nature. Even if you don't become a biologist, you can help others who are trying to conserve wildlife.

Q Where can I study to become a professional biologist?

A If you study biology at school, this will allow you to go to college or university – most of these teach biology. There are many different kinds of biology to choose from, such as marine biology, conservation biology, botany, zoology, agriculture and forestry.

Q When I've finished training, what kind of work can I do?

A You might be able to carry out scientific research that will take you to places such as tropical rainforests, where new species can be found.

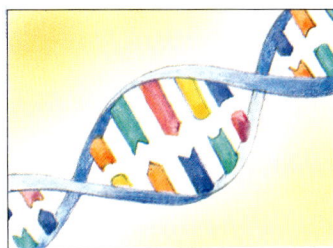

Q How can I find out about exotic plants and animals?

A You can buy or rent wildlife videos and CD-ROM disks, to see film of rare animals in exotic places. You can also use computer communications systems to get information from natural history museums and botanic gardens - pictures of the Wollemi pine have been sent around the world on the Internet.

You might carry out research into new techniques, such as genetic fingerprinting, that can help biologists to identify new animals.

Index